W9-AZM-135

The Greatest Bible Stories Ever Told
Amazing Miracles

Stephen Elkins

AUTHOR

Tim O'Connor

ILLUSTRATIONS

BROADMAN
& HOLMAN
PUBLISHERS

NASHVILLE, TENNESSEE

Copyright © 1999 by Stephen Elkins / Wonder Workshop, Inc.
Published in 2002 by Broadman & Holman Publishers
Nashville, Tennessee

Scripture quotations on pages 3, 11, 18, 21, 27, and 28 are from the
HOLY BIBLE, NEW INTERNATIONAL VERSION®,
copyright © 1973, 1978, 1984 by International Bible Society. Used by
permission of Zondervan Publishing House. All rights reserved.

Scripture quotation on page 15 is from the New American
Standard Bible, © the Lockman Foundation, 1960, 1962, 1963, 1971,
1972, 1973, 1975, 1977; used by permission.

Footprints On The Water (Stephen Elkins and Ronnie P. Kingery)
© 1996 Kenna Music (ASCAP). All rights reserved.
International copyright secured.

All other songs (except Public Domain) written, adapted, and/or arranged
by Stephen Elkins, © 1999 Wonder Workshop, Inc. All rights reserved.
International copyright secured.

Cover design and layout by Bill Farrar

A catalog record for the original Word & Song Bible
is available from the Library of Congress.

All rights reserved. Printed in Belgium.

ISBN 0-8054-2471-7

1 2 3 4 5   06 05 04 03 02

NOAH'S ARK

Genesis 9:13,15 I have set my rainbow in the clouds... (as a) sign of the covenant (promise). Never again will the waters become a flood to destroy all life.

Many years had passed since the day Adam and Eve were forced to leave the garden of Eden. The world was full of people who had become very wicked. They never prayed or thought about their Heavenly Father. God's heart became full of pain and He was sorry He had ever created them. So the Lord said, "I will destroy these people whom I have created."

But there was a man named Noah who loved the Lord with all his heart. When everyone else had become selfish and mean, Noah and his family walked with the Lord.

God was pleased with Noah and He said, "I am going to send a great flood upon the earth to destroy every living thing. Only you and your family will be saved."

God told Noah to build a large boat, called an ark, out of gopher wood. The ark would have many rooms and a roof over the top to keep out the water.

"The Lord said this ark should be 450 feet long, 75 feet wide and 45 feet tall, and have three decks. Now we're going to bring two of every kind of bird and beast, male and female, into this ark." Noah did all that God had asked him to do.

So Noah, together with his three sons Shem, Ham, and
Japheth, and his wife and his son's wives, built the ark.
They brought plenty of food aboard
for themselves and the
animals to eat.

Soon, the animals
came to Noah and were
loaded into the ark two by two. Then God said
to Noah, "Go into the ark, for it will rain in seven days."
Noah did all the Lord commanded.

Seven days soon passed. The skies darkened, the thunder crashed, and the rain began to fall. With two of every living creature aboard, God shut the door on Noah and his family. It rained for forty days and forty nights. The waters rose higher and higher floating the ark high above the earth. Every living thing perished. Only Noah and those with him in the ark were left.

The earth was flooded for 150 days. But God's watchcare was upon Noah and his family. God sent a warm heavenly breeze to dry the earth. Soon, the ark came to rest in the mountains of Ararat. Noah waited 40 days before he opened the window. He sent out a raven, but there was no dry place for the bird to land.

Then he sent out a dove, but the dove could find no dry place and returned to the ark. Noah waited seven more days before sending the dove out again. This time the dove returned with an olive leaf in its beak ... a sign that there was dry land. Noah waited seven more days and again sent the dove out, but this time the dove did not return.

Then God said to Noah, "Come out of the ark with your wife and your sons and their wives and all the animals." Noah was thankful God had saved his family, so he built an altar to please the Lord. "Thank you Lord for saving my family. You are a wonderful God." God made a promise never again to destroy the world with flood waters. As a sign of His promise, He set a beautiful rainbow in the sky.

Affirmation: I will trust God's promises!

DONKEY TALK

Numbers 22:28a   Then the LORD opened the donkey's mouth.

The Israelites traveled on to the plain of Moab and camped near the Jordan River. The Moabites were frightened to see so many people. "What if they attack us?" they said. "We will be destroyed!" So the king of Moab sent messengers to find the prophet named Balaam. They asked Balaam to put a curse on the Israelites so the Moabites could defeat them in battle.

Balaam said, "Spend the night here. I will ask God what He wants me to do." That night, the Lord spoke to Balaam, "Do not go with these men. You must never curse My people who are blessed." When he told the messengers that the Lord would not allow him to curse the Israelites, they said, "Don't let God stop you from doing this. We will pay you lots of money." Balaam was tempted by what they were offering and said, "I'll ask God again."

The next day Balaam got up, saddled his donkey, and left with the messengers of Moab. God was very angry that Balaam had disobeyed. He sent an angel with a drawn sword to stand in the road to block the way. Balaam's donkey saw the angel and turned off the road into a field. Balaam beat his donkey for doing this. But he could not see the angel. This happened a second and third time until finally the Lord opened the donkey's mouth and she said to Balaam, "What have I done to you to make you beat me three times?"

Balaam could not believe his ears! "A talking donkey?" he said. "You are acting crazy. If I had a sword I'd kill you right here!" Then the Lord opened Balaam's eyes and he saw the angel of the Lord standing in the road with his sword drawn. "Your donkey saw me and turned away from me three times. If she had not, I would have killed you, for you have disobeyed the Lord, and I am sent to stop you."

Balaam said to the angel, "I have sinned. I will turn around and go back." The angel said, "Go on with these men, but speak only what I tell you." Balaam agreed and went on with the messengers to meet with the king of Moab. Instead of cursing the God of Israel, he praised the Lord again and again for His goodness and faithfulness.

The king was furious. "Go! I told you to curse my enemies, not bless them." Then the prophet Balaam told the king that Moab would soon be defeated, and out of Israel would come a great ruler. The king went away very sad.

Affirmation: I will praise the Lord for His goodness!

BLINDED BY THE LIGHT

Acts 2:21 Everyone who calls on the name of the Lord shall be saved.

Many of the Jewish religious leaders continued to treat the Christian believers in a very unkind way. Saul of Tarsus was probably the most unkind. He did not believe in the Lord Jesus. He had men and women who loved the Lord put in chains and taken away to terrible prisons.

One day as Saul and his friends were traveling to a city called Damascus, a very bright light suddenly shone around him. Then Saul heard a voice from heaven saying, "Saul, why are you so unkind to Me?" When Saul asked, "Who are You, Lord?" He heard the voice reply, "I am Jesus." Then Saul knew that Jesus really was alive!

The light was so brilliant that it blinded Saul. Trembling with fear Saul asked, "Lord, what do You want me to do?"

The Lord commanded him to go to Damascus, and Saul obeyed.

Three dark days later, God sent a good man named Ananias to visit Saul. Suddenly, he could see again! Saul praised God as Ananias told him about God's special plan for his life. Later, Saul even changed his name from Saul to Paul, for now he would live for Jesus.

Affirmation: I will live for Jesus!

THE RED SEA MIRACLE

Exodus 14:14 The Lord will fight for you; you need only to be still.

After God sent the tenth and final plague upon the Egyptians, the plague on the first-born, the children of Israel were able to escape Pharaoh's harsh rule. Six hundred thousand men, plus women and children, set off for the promised land. To guide Moses and the Israelites, the Lord sent a huge pillar of clouds to follow during the day, and a great pillar of fire as a guiding light by night.

As soon as the Israelites left Egypt, Pharaoh's heart was quick to change his mind once again. "What have we done? We must capture the Israelites so they can work for us again."

Pharaoh took six hundred of his fastest chariots and an army of soldiers to capture the Israelites. As Moses reached the shores of the Red Sea, the Israelites saw the army coming. They were terrified. "We will die here in the desert," they cried.

Moses shouted, "Stand firm and do not be afraid. The Lord will fight for you." Then Moses lifted his staff and the seas parted. It was a miracle! The children of Israel walked through the sea with the walls of water all around them.

The Egyptian army followed Moses into the wall of water. But when morning came, the Lord threw the Egyptian army into confusion. The wheels on their chariots broke.

When the Israelites reached the other side, Moses stretched out his staff over the Red Sea. The powerful waters crashed down on top of the Egyptian army. They were defeated. Then the people of Israel put their trust in God.

Affirmation: I serve a God of miracles!

JOSHUA'S SHOUT!

Joshua 24:15 Choose ... this day whom you will serve ... but as for me and my household, we will serve the Lord.

After Moses died, the Lord spoke to Joshua saying, "Get ready to cross the Jordan River. The promised land awaits you. I will walk with you, Joshua, as I did with Moses. I will make you a strong leader, so be courageous and obey My laws."

Joshua shouted to the people, "Get ready, for in three days we cross the Jordan River into the promised land!"

At that time there were people already living in Canaan. Joshua knew that he must defeat them if they were going to possess the land. Wisely, he sent two spies into the great walled city of Jericho. Soon, he would know their strength and if they were preparing for battle.

The two spies secretly crossed the Jordan and entered Jericho. They stayed with a woman named Rahab, but the king soon found out!

He sent messengers to Rahab who said, "Bring out the two men who are spying on us. We know they're here!" Secretly, Rahab had hidden the two men on the roof of her house. "They were here, but they're gone. Perhaps you can catch them on the road if you hurry."

Just before nightfall, Rahab went back to the roof and said to the spies, "I have helped you, now you must help me. I know that the Lord is mighty and He has given this land to you."

"When the battle comes, save me and my family."
The men agreed that if Rahab would not tell the king
about them, they would save her family. Rahab's
house was part of the great wall, so that night the
men climbed out of Rahab's window, down a long
rope and escaped into the hills. The spies returned
to Joshua, "The Lord is surely giving our people this
land. The Canaanites are afraid of us!"

Three days later, Joshua said to the people,
"Tomorrow we cross the Jordan River. The ark of the
Lord will go before you. Follow behind it, for great is
our Lord!" Then came another miracle. As soon as
the priests carrying the ark set foot in the rushing
current of the Jordan River, the waters stopped
flowing. The Israelites could then pass through the
river on dry ground. God had made a way like He
had done at the Red Sea! Not until the last person
came out of the river did the waters flow again.

As Joshua neared the city of Jericho, he met a
strange man with his sword drawn. Joshua went to
him and said, "Are you for us or against us?"

"I command the invisible army of the Lord," he
replied. Joshua fell facedown with fear and respect.
Then the Lord told Joshua what he must do to win
the coming battle.

The day of the battle came. Seven priests blowing seven trumpets marched around the city of Jericho one time. The ark of the Lord was right behind them. An armed guard marched ahead of the priests and followed up behind the ark. They circled Jericho once and no one spoke a single word. "What are they doing?" cried the people of Jericho. "God is going to destroy us!"
They were afraid.

God commanded Joshua and his army to march around the city each day for six days. On the seventh day, the people marched around Jericho seven times. But the seventh time, just as the priests sounded the trumpet blast, Joshua commanded the nation, "Shout! For the Lord has given you the city! Shout! Shout!"

The people shouted
and the trumpets blasted, louder
and louder, until the walls of Jericho began to crack
and came tumbling down! The city was captured. Rahab
and her family who had helped them were saved.

Affirmation: The Lord is mighty!

JESUS HEALS PETER'S MOTHER-IN-LAW

Mark 1:30   Simon's mother-in-law was in bed with a fever, and they told Jesus about her.

Simon, also called Peter, was one of Jesus' disciples. One day Peter came to Jesus and told Him about his mother-in-law who was very sick. Mark writes: "Together they went to her bed where she lay with a terrible fever. Jesus reached out and gently took her by the hand. With His touch, the fever suddenly left her. She was healed by the miracle touch of Jesus!"

Affirmation: I will call upon the Lord to heal me!

FOOTPRINTS ON THE WATER

Mark 6:50 Take courage! It is I. Don't be afraid.

Jesus asked the disciples to sail ahead to Bethsaida while He said goodbye to the crowds. After they had gone, He went into the hills alone to pray.

When evening came, a mighty wind blew across the lake. The disciples could hardly row. Mark writes, "Jesus saw their trouble and went out to them, walking on the water!"

When they saw something coming toward them, they thought it was a ghost. They were very frightened! Then Jesus shouted, "It is I ... don't be afraid!" Peter said, "Lord, if it's You, tell me to come to You on the water." Jesus commanded, "Come."

Peter stepped out of the boat and walked to Jesus. But the mighty wind and the waves caused him to be afraid and lose faith. Then he began to sink.
"Lord save me!"
cried Peter.

Jesus reached out His hand and caught Peter. "Why did you doubt?" asked Jesus. Then they both climbed into the boat.

All the men worshiped Jesus saying, "Truly You are the Son of God!"

Affirmation: I will trust Jesus for a miracle!

COLLECT ALL 10

Word & Song
AUDIO BOOK

The Greatest Bible Stories Ever Told
Amazing Miracles
Narrated by
ROY CLARK · KAY DeKALB SMITH
STEVE & ANNIE CHAPMAN · LLOYD OGILVIE
AGES 3-10
0-8054-2471-7

The Greatest Bible Stories Ever Told
God's Power
Narrated by
LLOYD OGILVIE · DEAN STONE
GEORGE BEVERLY SHEA
AGES 3-10
0-8054-2466-0

The Greatest Bible Stories Ever Told
Stories of Faith
Narrated by
LARNELLE HARRIS
STEVE & ANNIE CHAPMAN · LLOYD OGILVIE
AGES 3-10
0-8054-2470-9

The Greatest Bible Stories Ever Told
Stories that
Build Character
Narrated by
LARNELLE HARRIS · STEVE GREEN
LLOYD OGILVIE
AGES 3-10
0-8054-2469-5

The Greatest Bible Stories Ever Told
Children in the Bible
Narrated by
MAX LUCADO · LARNELLE HARRIS
LLOYD OGILVIE · KAY DeKALB SMITH
AGES 3-10
0-8054-2474-1

The Greatest Bible Stories Ever Told
Courage & Strength
Narrated by
REGGIE WHITE · LARNELLE HARRIS
STEVE GREEN · LLOYD OGILVIE · STEVE CAMP
AGES 3-10
0-8054-2468-7

The Greatest Bible Stories Ever Told
Friendship & Kindness
Narrated by
MAX LUCADO · REBECCA ST JAMES
LARNELLE HARRIS · TWILA PARIS · STEVE GREEN
AGES 3-10
0-8054-2473-3

The Greatest Bible Stories Ever Told
The Good Shepherd
Narrated by
STEVE GREEN
JERRY FALWELL · ANNIE CHAPMAN
AGES 3-10
0-8054-2475-x

The Greatest Bible Stories Ever Told
Prayer & Promise
Narrated by
MAX LUCADO · GEORGE BEVERLY SHEA
STEVE GREEN · ADRIAN ROGERS · LLOYD OGILVIE
AGES 3-10
0-8054-2472-5

The Greatest Bible Stories Ever Told
Special Families
JONI EARECKSON TADA · TWILA PARIS · STEVE GREEN
LLOYD OGILVIE · STEVE & ANNIE CHAPMAN
AGES 3-10
0-8054-2467-9

Available in Your Favorite Christian Bookstore.

We hope you enjoyed this Word & Song Storybook.